Pebble®
Plus

Pet Cats UP CLOSE

by Gillia M. Olson

Gail Saunders-Smith, PhD, Consulting Editor

CAPSTONE PRESS
a capstone imprint

Pebble Plus is published by Capstone Press,
1710 Roe Crest Drive, North Mankato, Minnesota 56003
www.capstonepub.com

Library of Congress Cataloging-in-Publication Data
Olson, Gillia M.
Pet Cats Up Close / by Gillia M. Olson.
pages cm.—(Pebble Plus. Pets Up Close)
Includes bibliographical references and index.
Summary: "Full-color, zoomed-in photos and simple text describe pet cats' body parts"—Provided by publisher.
Audience: Ages 5–8.
Audience: Grades K to 3.
ISBN 978-1-4914-0582-6 (hardcover)
ISBN 978-1-4914-0616-8 (ebook pdf)
1. Cats—Juvenile literature. I. Title.
SF445.7.O56 2015
636.8—dc23
2014012293

Editorial Credits
Jeni Wittrock, editor; Bobbie Nuytten, designer; Svetlana Zhurkin, media researcher; Katy LaVigne, production specialist

Photo Credits
Dreamstime: Pjatochka, 5; Shutterstock: 9744444159, 17, ANCH, 11, Ann Precious (paw prints), back cover and throughout, ArtTDi, cover, Birute Vijeikiene, 21, dimmitrius, 9, Ekaterina Shvaygert, 7, Glen Robinson, 13, Olanka, 15, Renata Apanaviciene, 1, Tony Campbell, 19

Note to Parents and Teachers

The Pets Up Close set supports national science standards related to life science. This book describes and illustrates pet cats. The images support early readers in understanding the text. The repetition of words and phrases helps early readers learn new words. This book also introduces early readers to subject-specific vocabulary words, which are defined in the Glossary section. Early readers may need assistance to read some words and to use the Table of Contents, Glossary, Read More, Internet Sites, and Index sections of the book.

Printed in the United States of America in North Mankato, Minnesota.
042014   008087CGF14

Table of Contents

Fantastic Felines

Watch out for flying cats!

Cats have cool body parts to

help them leap, play, and hunt.

Let's get an up close look

at these furry friends.

Cat Eyes

Cat eyes reflect light
to help them see in the dark.
Cats use their good eyesight
to hunt at night.

Cat Whiskers

In the dark, cats use whiskers to feel around and find prey. A cat has 24 whiskers on its upper lip. Whiskers grow on its chin and eyebrows too.

9

Cat Ears

Cats hear better than people and even dogs. Cats can turn their ears toward sounds to hear better. They might hear prey before they see it.

11

Cat Tongues

Cats have tiny barbs
on their tongues. Cat tongues
can rasp meat from bones.
Tongues also make grooming
easier by acting like a brush.

13

Cat Noses

Cats use their noses to sniff out prey. Inside a cat's mouth is a Jacobson's organ. This organ lets cats sense even more smells.

Cat Claws

Cats can pull in their claws.

The claws stay sharp,

instead of wearing down

on the ground. Pulled-in claws

make for quiet hunting too.

Cat Tails

A cat's tail helps it balance on narrow ledges and make sudden turns. Cats are graceful because of their terrific tails.

19

Cat Fur

A cat's fur protects it
from cold and hot weather.
Cats can have short, long,
or curly fur. But the best fur
is the kind you get to pet.

Glossary

barb—a hook-shaped part

groom—to clean and make an animal look neat

Jacobson's organ—an organ on the roof of the mouth of a cat; the tongue picks up scents and carries them to the Jacobson's organ

ledge—a narrow shelf that sticks out from a wall

prey—an animal hunted by other animals for food

protect—to keep safe

rasp—to rub as if with a rough file with pointy ends

reflect—to return light from an object

Read More

Armentrout, David and Patricia. *Kitty Care.* Let's Talk About Pets. Vero Beach, Fla.: Rourke Pub., 2011.

Heneghan, Judith. *Love Your Cat.* New York: Windmill Books, 2013.

Hutmacher, Kimberly M. *I Want a Cat.* I Want a Pet. Mankato, Minn.: Capstone Press, 2012.

Internet Sites

FactHound offers a safe, fun way to find Internet sites related to this book. All of the sites on FactHound have been researched by our staff.

Here's all you do:

Visit *www.facthound.com*

Type in this code: 9781491405826

Super-cool stuff!

Check out projects, games and lots more at
www.capstonekids.com

Index

Word Count: 224
Grade: 1
Early-Intervention Level: 16